CHRISTMAS CAROLS
FOR OCARINA

ISBN 978-1-5400-2923-2

HAL•LEONARD®

Visit Hal Leonard Online at
www.halleonard.com

Contact Us:
Hal Leonard
7777 West Bluemound Road
Milwaukee, WI 53213
Email: info@halleonard.com

In Europe contact:
Hal Leonard Europe Limited
Distribution Centre, Newmarket Road
Bury St Edmunds, Suffolk, IP33 3YB
Email: info@halleonardeurope.com

In Australia contact:
Hal Leonard Australia Pty. Ltd.
4 Lentara Court
Cheltenham, Victoria, 3192 Australia
Email: info@halleonard.com.au

T0061505

CONTENTS

ANGELS FROM THE REALMS OF GLORY

Words by JAMES MONTGOMERY
Music by HENRY T. SMART

Moderately

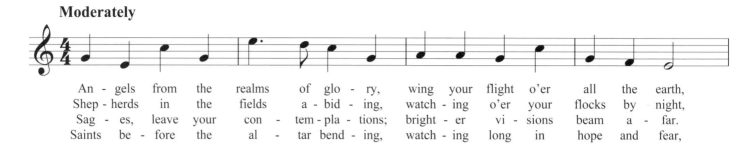

An - gels from the realms of glo - ry, wing your flight o'er all the earth,
Shep - herds in the fields a - bid - ing, watch - ing o'er your flocks by night,
Sag - es, leave your con - tem - pla - tions; bright - er vi - sions beam a - far.
Saints be - fore the al - tar bend - ing, watch - ing long in hope and fear,

ye who sang cre - a - tion's sto - ry, now pro - claim Mes - si - ah's birth.
God with man is now re - sid - ing; yon - der shines the ___ in - fant Light.
Seek the great de - sire of na - tions; ye have seen His ___ na - tal star.
sud - den - ly the Lord, de - scend - ing, in His tem - ple ___ shall ap - pear.

Come and wor - ship! Come and wor - ship! Wor - ship Christ the new - born King!

ANGELS WE HAVE HEARD ON HIGH

Traditional French Carol
Translated by JAMES CHADWICK

Joyfully

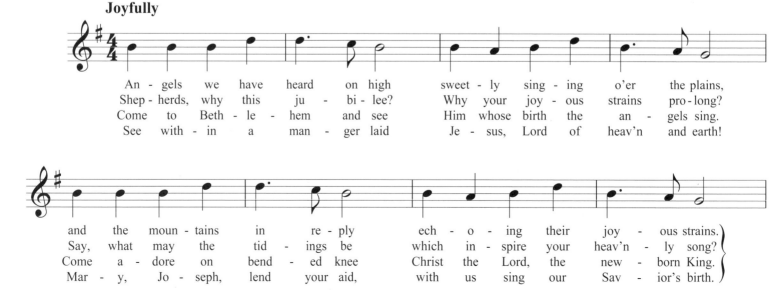

An - gels we have heard on high sweet - ly sing - ing o'er the plains,
Shep - herds, why this ju - bi - lee? Why your joy - ous strains pro - long?
Come to Beth - le - hem and see Him whose birth the an - gels sing.
See with - in a man - ger laid Je - sus, Lord of heav'n and earth!

and the moun - tains in re - ply ech - o - ing their joy - ous strains.
Say, what may the tid - ings be which in - spire your heav'n - ly song?
Come a - dore on bend - ed knee Christ the Lord, the new - born King.
Mar - y, Jo - seph, lend your aid, with us sing our Sav - ior's birth.

Glo - - - ri - a in ex - cel - sis De - o. Glo - - - ri - a in ex - cel - sis De - o.

AS WITH GLADNESS MEN OF OLD

Words by WILLIAM CHATTERTON DIX
Music by CONRAD KOCHER

Moderately fast

As with __ glad - ness men of old did the guid - ing star be - hold;
As with __ joy - ful steps they sped to that low - ly man - ger bed,
As they __ of - fered gifts most rare at that man - ger rude and bare,
Ho - ly __ Je - sus, ev - 'ry day keep us in the nar - row way;

as with __ joy they hailed its light, lead - ing on - ward, beam - ing bright;
there to __ bend the knee be - fore Him whom heav'n and earth a - dore;
so may __ we with ho - ly joy, pure and free from sin's al - loy,
and when __ earth - ly things are past, bring our ran - somed souls at last

so, most gra - cious Lord, may we ev - er - more be led to Thee.
so may we with will - ing feet ev - er seek Thy mer - cy seat.
all our cost - liest trea - sures bring, Christ, to Thee, our heav'n - ly King.
where they need no star to guide, where no clouds Thy glo - ry hide.

AULD LANG SYNE

Words by ROBERT BURNS
Traditional Scottish Melody

Should auld ac-quaint-ance be for-got, and nev-er brought to mind? Should

auld ac-quaint-ance be for-got and days of Auld Lang Syne? For

Auld _____ Lang _____ Syne, my dear, for Auld _____ Lang _____ Syne, we'll

tak' a cup o' kind-ness yet, for _____ Auld _____ Lang _____ Syne.

AWAY IN A MANGER

Words by JOHN T. McFARLAND (v.3)
Music by JAMES R. MURRAY

A - way in a man - ger, no crib for a bed, the
The cat - tle are low - ing, the Ba - by a - wakes, but
Be near me, Lord Je - sus, I ask Thee to stay close

lit - tle Lord Je - sus laid down His sweet head. The
lit - tle Lord Je - sus no cry - ing He makes. I
by me for - ev - er, and love me, I pray. Bless

stars in the sky _____ looked down where He lay, the
love Thee, Lord Je - sus, look down from the sky, and
all the dear chil - dren in Thy ten - der care, and

lit - tle Lord Je - sus, a - sleep on the hay.
stay by my cra - dle till morn - ing is nigh.
take us to heav - en to live with Thee there.

COVENTRY CAROL

Words by ROBERT CROO
Traditional English Melody

Tenderly

1. Lul - lay, Thou lit - tle ti - ny Child, by, by, lul - ly, lul - lay. _____ Lul - lay, Thou lit - tle ti - ny Child, by, by, lul - ly lul - lay. _____
2. O sis - ters too, how may we do, for to pre - serve this day. _____ This poor Young - ling for whom we sing, by, by, lul - ly lul - lay. _____

3., 4. *(See additional lyrics)*

Additional Lyrics

3. Herod, the King
   In his raging,
   Charged he hath this day.
   His men of might,
   In his own sight,
   All young children to slay.

4. That woe is me,
   Poor child for thee!
   And ever morn and day,
   For thy parting
   Neither say nor sing
   By, by, lully, lullay.

DECK THE HALL

Traditional Welsh Carol

Brightly

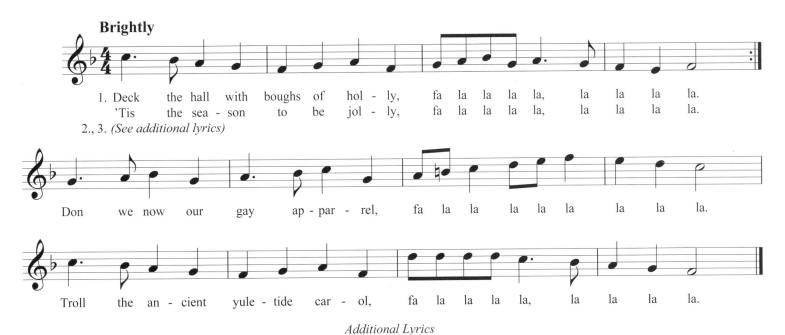

1. Deck the hall with boughs of hol - ly, fa la la la la, la la la la.
   'Tis the sea - son to be jol - ly, fa la la la la, la la la la.

2., 3. *(See additional lyrics)*

Don we now our gay ap - par - rel, fa la la la la la la la la.

Troll the an - cient yule - tide car - ol, fa la la la la, la la la la.

Additional Lyrics

2. See the blazing Yule before us, fa la la la la, la la la la.
   Strike the harp and join the chorus, fa la la la la, la la la la.
   Follow me in merry measure, fa la la la la la la la la.
   While I tell of Yuletide treasure, fa la la la la, la la la la.

3. Fast away the old year passes, fa la la la la, la la la la.
   Hail the new, ye lads and lasses, fa la la la la, la la la la.
   Sing we joyous all together, fa la la la la la la la la.
   Heedless of the wind and weather, fa la la la la, la la la la.

DING DONG! MERRILY ON HIGH!

French Carol

Ding dong! Mer-ri-ly on high in heav'n the bells are ring-ing.
E'en so here be-low, be-low, let stee-ple bells be swung-en,
Pray you, du-ti-ful-ly prime your mat-in chime, ye ring-ers.

Ding dong! Ver-i-ly the sky is riv'n with an-gel sing-ing.
and i-o, i-o, i-o, by priest and peo-ple sung-en.
May you beau-ti-ful-ly rime your eve-time some, ye sing-ers.

Glo - - - - ri-a, Ho-san-na in ex-cel-sis!

THE FIRST NOEL

17th Century English Carol
Music from W. Sandys' *Christmas Carols*

The __ first ____ no - el the __ an - gel did say was to

cer - tain poor shep - herds in fields as they lay; in ___ fields ____ where _

they lay __ keep - ing their sheep on a cold win - ter's night ___ that

was ___ so deep. No - el, ___ No - el, No - el, No -

el, born is the King ___ of Is - ra - el.

GO, TELL IT ON THE MOUNTAIN

African-American Spiritual
Verses by JOHN W. WORK, Jr., 1907

Brightly

Go, tell it on the moun - tain, o - ver the hills and ev - 'ry - where.

Last time Fine

Go, tell it on the moun - tain that Je - sus Christ ___ is born.

{ While
  The
  Down

shep - herds kept their watch - ing o'er si - lent flocks by night, be -
shep - herds feared and trem - bled when, lo! a - bove the earth rang
in a low - ly man - ger the hum - ble Christ was born, and

D.C.

hold, through - out the heav - ens there shone a ho - ly light. _____
out the an - gel cho - rus that hailed our Sav - ior's birth. _____
God sent us sal - va - tion that bless - ed Christ - mas morn. _____

GOOD KING WENCESLAS

Words by JOHN M. NEALE
Music from *Piae Cantiones*

Quickly

Good King Wen - ces - las looked out on the feast of Ste - phen,

when the snow lay 'round a - bout, deep, and crisp, and e - ven.

Bright - ly shone the moon that night, though the frost was cru - el,

when a poor man came in sight, gath -'ring win - ter fu - el.

GOD REST YE MERRY, GENTLEMEN

Traditional English Carol

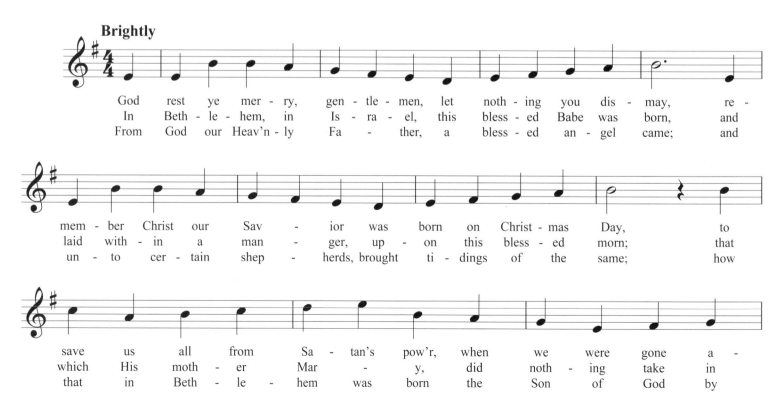

Brightly

God rest ye mer - ry, gen - tle - men, let noth - ing you dis - may, re -
In Beth - le - hem, in Is - ra - el, this bless - ed Babe was born, and
From God our Heav'n - ly Fa - ther, a bless - ed an - gel came; and

mem - ber Christ our Sav - ior was born on Christ - mas Day, to
laid with - in a man - ger, up - on this bless - ed morn; that
un - to cer - tain shep - herds, brought ti - dings of the same; how

save us all from Sa - tan's pow'r, when we were gone a -
which His moth - er Mar - y, did noth - ing take in
that in Beth - le - hem was born the Son of God by

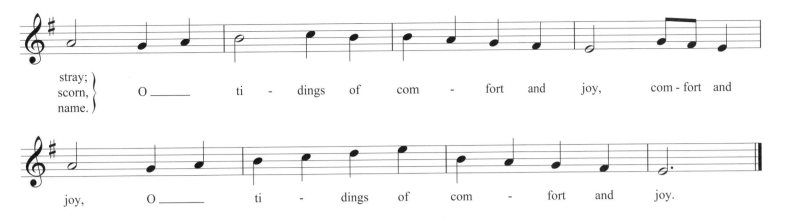

stray;
scorn, } O ____ ti - dings of com - fort and joy, com - fort and
name.

joy, O ____ ti - dings of com - fort and joy.

HARK! THE HERALD ANGELS SING

Words by CHARLES WESLEY
Altered by GEORGE WHITEFIELD
Music by FELIX MENDELSSOHN-BARTHOLDY
Arranged by WILLIAM H. CUMMINGS

Moderately

Hark! The her - ald an - gels sing, ___ "Glo - ry to the new - born King!
Christ, by high - est heav'n a - dored, ___ Christ, the ev - er - last - ing Lord,
Hail, the heav'n - born Prince of Peace! ___ Hail, the Sun of Right - eous - ness!

Peace on Earth, and mer - cy mild, ___ God and sin - ners re - con - ciled!"
Late in time be - hold Him come, ___ off - spring of the vir - gin's womb.
Light and life to all He brings, ___ ris'n with heal - ing in His wings.

Joy - ful all ye na - tions, rise, ___ join the tri - umph of the skies, ___
Veil'd in flesh the God - head see: ___ hail th'in - car - nate De - i - ty, ___
Mild He lays His glo - ry by, ___ born that man no more may die, ___

with th'an - gel - ic host pro - claim, "Christ is ___ born in Beth - le - hem!"}
pleased as Man with men to dwell, Je - sus ___ our Em - man - u - el!
born to raise the sons of earth, born to ___ give them sec - ond birth.

Hark! The her - ald an - gels sing, "Glo - ry ___ to the new - born King!"

IT CAME UPON THE MIDNIGHT CLEAR

Words by EDMUND HAMILTON SEARS
Music by RICHARD STORRS WILLIS

JINGLE BELLS

Words and Music by
J. PIERPONT

JOY TO THE WORLD

Words by ISAAC WATTS
Music by GEORGE FRIDERIC HANDEL

Brightly

Joy to the world! The Lord is come; let Earth re - ceive her King. _____
Joy to the earth! The Sav - ior reigns; let men their songs em - ploy. _____
No more let sins and sor - rows grow, nor thorns in - fest the ground. _____
He rules the world with truth and grace, and makes the na - tions prove _____

_____ Let ev - 'ry _____ heart _____ pre - pare _____ Him _____ room. _____ And heav'n and na - ture _____
_____ While fields and _____ floods, _____ rocks, hills _____ and _____ plains, _____ re - peat the sound - ing _____
_____ He comes to _____ make _____ His bless - ings _____ flow _____ far as the curse is _____
_____ the glo - ries _____ of _____ His right - eous - ness, _____ and won - ders of His _____

sing, and _ heav'n and na - ture _ sing, and _ heav'n _ and heav'n _____ and na - ture sing.
joy, re - peat the sound-ing _ joy, re - peat, _____ re - peat _____ the sound - ing joy.
found, far _ as the curse is _ found, far as, _____ far as _____ the curse is found.
love, and _ won-ders of His _ love, and _ won - ders, won - ders of His love.

O CHRISTMAS TREE

Traditional German Carol

Moderately

O Christ - mas tree! O Christ - mas tree, you stand in ver - dant beau - ty! O

Christ - mas tree! O Christ - mas tree, you stand in ver - dant beau - ty! Your

boughs are green in sum - mer's glow, and do not fade in win - ter's snow. O

Christ - mas tree! O Christ - mas tree, You stand in ver - dant beau - ty!

O COME, O COME, EMMANUEL

Traditional Latin Text
V. 1,2 translated by JOHN M. NEALE
V. 3,4 translated by HENRY S. COFFIN
15th Century French Melody
Adapted by THOMAS HELMORE

Moderately slow, in 2

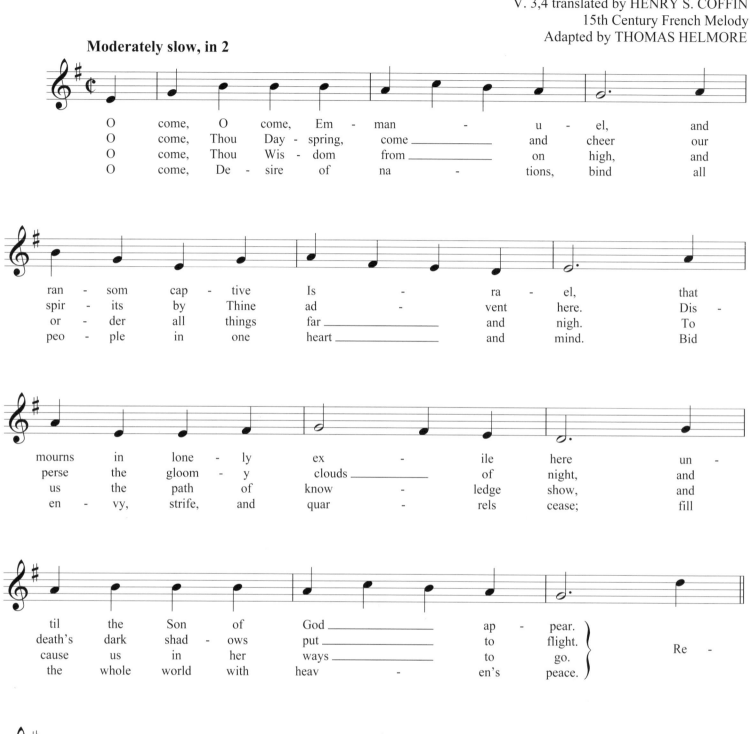

O   come, O   come, Em - man - u - el,   and
O   come, Thou Day - spring,   come _____   and   cheer   our
O   come, Thou Wis - dom   from _____   on   high,   and
O   come, De - sire of   na - tions,   bind   all

ran - som   cap - tive   Is - ra - el,   that
spir - its   by   Thine   ad - vent   here.   Dis -
or - der   all   things   far _____   and   nigh.   To
peo - ple   in   one   heart _____   and   mind.   Bid

mourns   in   lone - ly   ex - ile   here   un -
perse   the   gloom - y   clouds _____   of   night,   and
us   the   path   of   know - ledge   show,   and
en - vy,   strife,   and   quar - rels   cease;   fill

til   the   Son   of   God _____   ap - pear.
death's   dark   shad - ows   put _____   to   flight.
cause   us   in   her   ways _____   to   go.
the   whole   world   with   heav - en's   peace.   Re -

joice,   re - joice!   Em - man - u - el   shall

come   to   thee,   O   Is - ra - el!

O HOLY NIGHT

French Words by PLACIDE CAPPEAU
English Words by JOHN S. DWIGHT
Music by ADOLPHE ADAM

O COME, ALL YE FAITHFUL

Music by JOHN FRANCIS WADE
Latin Words translated by FREDERICK OAKELEY

O come all ye faith - ful, joy - ful and tri - um - phant, O
Sing, choirs of an - gels, sing in ex - ul - ta - tion, ___
Yea, Lord, we greet Thee, Born this hap - py morn - ing, ___

come ye, O come ___ ye to Beth - le - hem.
sing all ye cit - i - zens of heav'n ___ a - bove.
Je - sus, to Thee ___ be all glo - ry giv'n.

Come and be - hold Him, born the King of an - gels
Glo - ry to God ___ in ___ the ___ high - est. } O
Word of the Fa - ther, now in flesh ap - pear - ing.

come let us a - dore Him, O come let us a - dore Him, O

come let us a - dore Him, ___ Christ ___ the Lord.

O LITTLE TOWN OF BETHLEHEM

Words by PHILLIPS BROOKS
Music by LEWIS H. REDNER

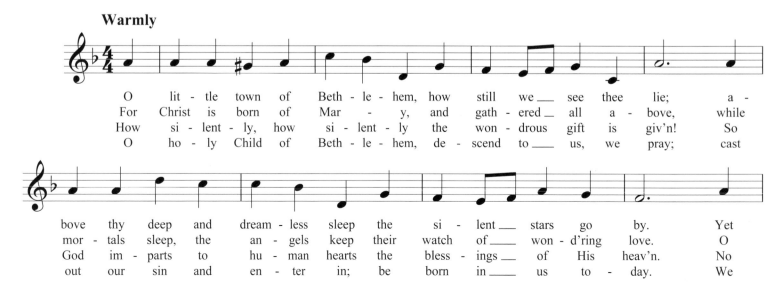

O lit - tle town of Beth - le - hem, how still we ___ see thee lie; a -
For Christ is born of Mar - y, and gath - ered ___ all a - bove, while
How si - lent - ly, how si - lent - ly the won - drous gift is giv'n! So
O ho - ly Child of Beth - le - hem, de - scend to ___ us, we pray; cast

bove thy deep and dream - less sleep the si - lent ___ stars go by. Yet
mor - tals sleep, the an - gels keep their watch of ___ won - d'ring love. O
God im - parts to hu - man hearts the bless - ings ___ of His heav'n. No
out our sin and en - ter in; be born in ___ us to - day. We

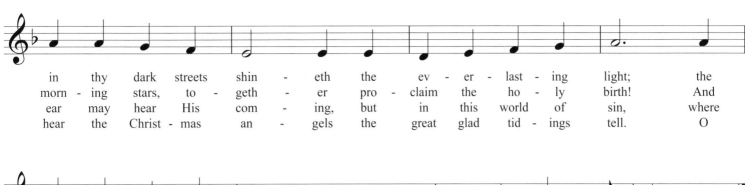

ONCE IN ROYAL DAVID'S CITY

Words by CECIL F. ALEXANDER
Music by HENRY J. GAUNTLETT

SILENT NIGHT

Words by JOSEPH MOHR
Translated by JOHN F. YOUNG
Music by FRANZ X. GRUBER

Slowly, in 6

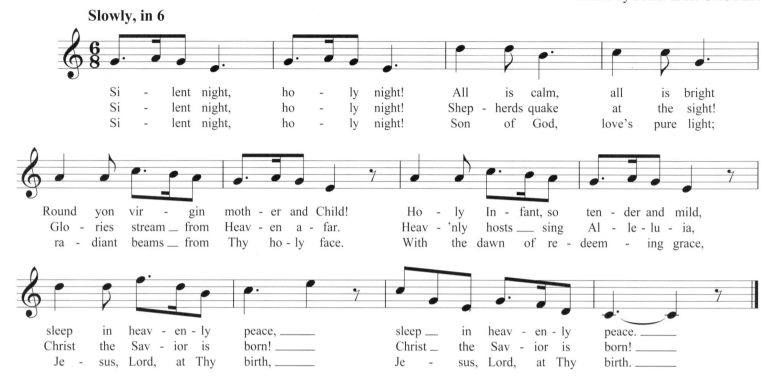

Si - lent night, ho - ly night! All is calm, all is bright
Si - lent night, ho - ly night! Shep - herds quake at the sight!
Si - lent night, ho - ly night! Son of God, love's pure light;

Round yon vir - gin moth - er and Child! Ho - ly In - fant, so ten - der and mild,
Glo - ries stream from Heav - en a - far. Heav - 'nly hosts sing Al - le - lu - ia,
ra - diant beams from Thy ho - ly face. With the dawn of re - deem - ing grace,

sleep in heav - en - ly peace, sleep in heav - en - ly peace.
Christ the Sav - ior is born! Christ the Sav - ior is born!
Je - sus, Lord, at Thy birth, Je - sus, Lord, at Thy birth.

TOYLAND
from BABES IN TOYLAND

Words by GLEN MacDONOUGH
Music by VICTOR HERBERT

Slowly, in 2

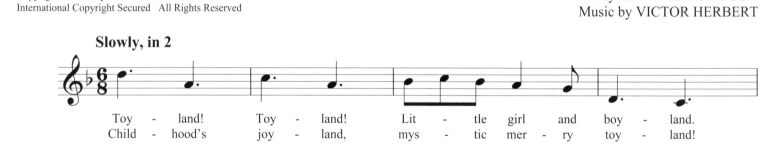

Toy - land! Toy - land! Lit - tle girl and boy - land.
Child - hood's joy - land, mys - tic mer - ry toy - land!

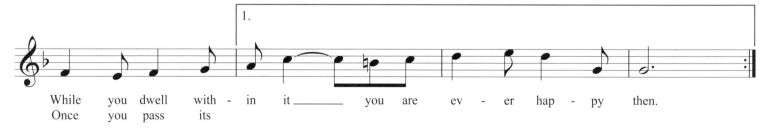

1.
While you dwell with - in it you are ev - er hap - py then.
Once you pass its

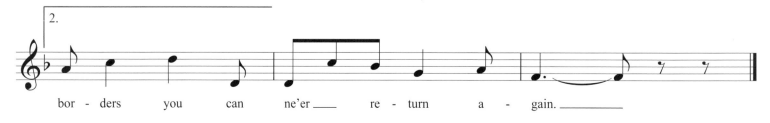

2.
bor - ders you can ne'er re - turn a - gain.

THE TWELVE DAYS OF CHRISTMAS

Traditional English Carol

Moderately
Verse 1

On the first day of Christ-mas my true love gave to me: a par - tridge in a pear tree.

Verses 2-4

On the sec - ond day of Christ-mas my true love gave to me: two tur - tle doves,
third __ day of Christ-mas my true love gave to me: three French __ hens, } and a par-tridge __ in a pear tree.
fourth __ day of Christ-mas my true love gave to me: four call - ing birds,

Verse 5

On the fifth day of Christ - mas my true love gave to me: five gold - en rings.

Four __ call-ing birds, three French hens, two __ tur - tle doves, and a par - tridge __ in a pear tree.

Verses 6-12

On the sixth day of Christ-mas my true love gave to me: six geese a - lay - ing.
On the sev-enth day of Christ-mas my true love gave to me: sev-en swans a - swim - ing,
On the eighth day of Christ-mas my true love gave to me: eight maids a - milk - ing.
On the ninth day of Christ-mas my true love gave to me: nine lad - ies danc - ing, } five gold - en
On the tenth day of Christ-mas my true love gave to me: ten lords a - leap - ing,
On the 'lev-enth day of Christ-mas my true love gave to me: 'lev-en pip - ers - pip - ing,
On the twelfth day of Christ-mas my true love gave to me: twelve drum-mers drum-ming,

rings. Four __ call-ing birds, three French hens, two __ tur-tle doves, and a par - tridge __ in a pear tree.

These bars are played a different number of times for each verse.

UKRAINIAN BELL CAROL

Traditional
Music by MYKOLA LEONTOVYCH

UP ON THE HOUSETOP

Words and Music by
B.R. HANBY

Brightly

Up on the house-top __ rein-deer pause, out jumps good old San-ta Claus;

down through the chim-ney with lots of toys, all for the lit-tle ones, Christ-mas joys.

Ho, ho, ho! Who would-n't go? Ho, ho, ho! Who would-n't go? __

Up on the house-top, click, click, click. Down through the chim-ney with good Saint Nick.

WHAT CHILD IS THIS?

Words by WILLIAM C. DIX
16th Century English Melody

Moderately slow

What Child is this, __ who, laid to rest, __ on Mar-y's lap __ is

sleep - ing? When an-gels greet __ with an-thems sweet __ while shep-herds

watch __ are keep - ing? This, this __ is Christ the King, __ whom

shep - herds guard __ and an - gels sing; haste, haste __ to

bring him laud, __ The babe, __ the son __ of Mar - y.

WE THREE KINGS OF ORIENT ARE

Words and Music by
JOHN H. HOPKINS, JR.

Moderately fast

We three kings of O - ri - ent are, bear - ing gifts we tra - verse a - far,
Born a King on Beth - le - hem's plain, gold I bring to crown Him a - gain,
Frank - in - cense to of - fer have I, in - cense owns a De - i - ty nigh.
Myrrh is mine, its bit - ter per - fume breathes a life of gath - er - ing gloom;
Glo - rious now, be - hold Him a - rise, King and God and Sac - ri - fice!

field and foun - tain, moor and moun - tain, fol - low - ing yon - der star.
King for - ev - er, ceas - ing nev - er, o - ver us all to reign.
Prayer and prais - ing, all men rais - ing, wor - ship Him God on high.
sor - r'wing, sigh - ing, bleed - ing, dy - ing, sealed in the stone - cold tomb.
Al - le - lu - ia, Al - le - lu - ia, Earth to heav'n re - plies.
O _____

star of won - der, star of night, star with roy - al beau - ty bright.

West - ward lead - ing, still pro - ceed - ing, guide us to thy per - fect light.

WE WISH YOU A MERRY CHRISTMAS

Traditional English Folksong

Gaily

We wish you a mer - ry Christ - mas, we wish you a mer - ry Christ - mas, we

wish you a mer - ry Christ - mas, and a hap - py new year! Good tid - ings to you, wher -

ev - er you are! Good tid - ings for Christ - mas, and a hap - py new year!

12-Hole Ocarina Fingering Chart

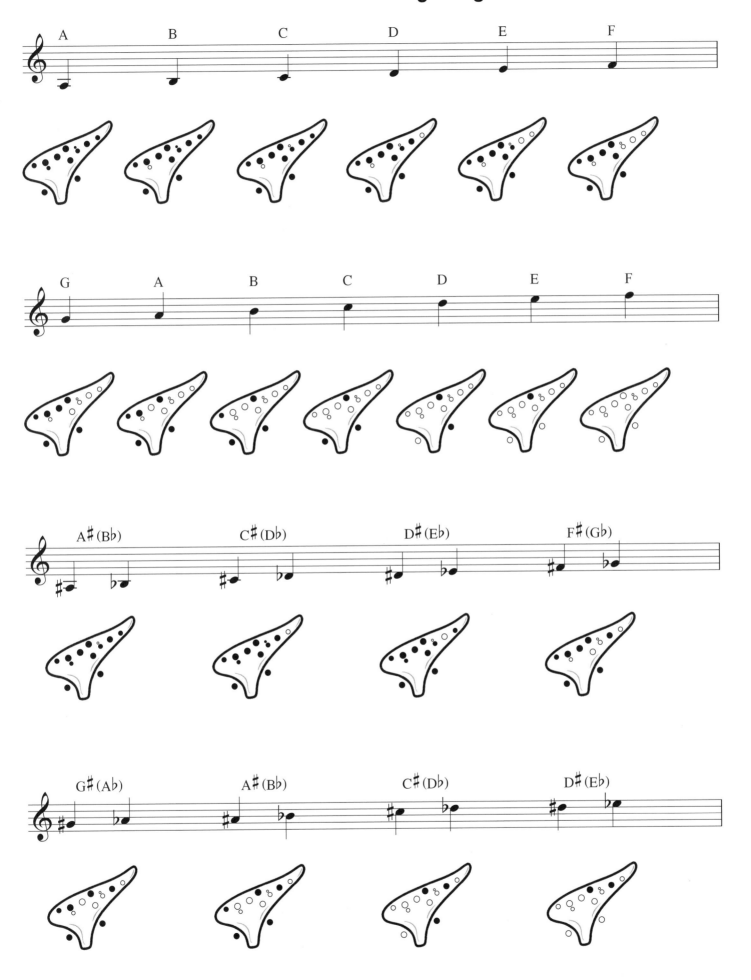

MORE GREAT OCARINA PUBLICATIONS

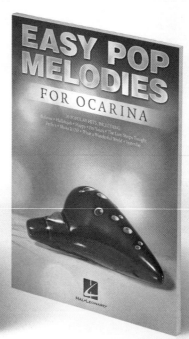

Hal Leonard Ocarina Method
by Cris Gale

The Hal Leonard Ocarina Method is a comprehensive, easy-to-use beginner's guide, designed for anyone just learning to play the ocarina. Inside you'll find loads of techniques, tips and fun songs to learn and play. The accompanying online video, featuring author Cris Gale, provides further instruction as well as demonstrations of the music in the book. Topics covered include: a history of the ocarina • types of ocarinas • breathing and articulation • note names and key signatures • meter signatures and rhythmic notation • fingering charts • many classic folksongs • and more.

00146676 Book/Online Video $12.99

Folk Songs for Ocarina
Arranged for 10-, 11-, and 12-hole ocarinas.

All the Pretty Little Horses • Alouette • Amazing Grace • Annie Laurie • Auld Lang Syne • Aura Lee • The Banana Boat Song • The Blue Bells of Scotland • Danny Boy • Follow the Drinkin' Gourd • Frere Jacques (Are You Sleeping?) • Greensleeves • Hava Nagila (Let's Be Happy) • Home on the Range • Hush, Little Baby • Joshua (Fit the Battle of Jericho) • Kumbaya • La Cucaracha • Little Brown Jug • Loch Lomond • My Bonnie Lies over the Ocean • My Old Kentucky Home • My Wild Irish Rose • Oh! Susanna • Old Dan Tucker • Sakura (Cherry Blossoms) • Scarborough Fair • Shenandoah • Simple Gifts • Skip to My Lou • Sometimes I Feel like a Motherless Child • Swing Low, Sweet Chariot • There Is a Balm in Gilead • This Little Light of Mine • Twinkle, Twinkle Little Star • Volga Boatman Song • Were You There? • When Johnny Comes Marching Home • When the Saints Go Marching In • Yankee Doodle • The Yellow Rose of Texas.

00276000.. $9.99

Prices, contents, and availability subject to change without notice.
Disney characters and artwork © Disney Enterprises, Inc.

Easy Pop Melodies for Ocarina
Arranged for 10-, 11-, and 12-hole ocarinas.

Believer • Candle in the Wind • City of Stars • Clocks • Edelweiss • Every Breath You Take • (Everything I Do) I Do It for You • Hallelujah • Happy • Hey, Soul Sister • I'm Yours • Let It Be • Let It Go • The Lion Sleeps Tonight • Morning Has Broken • My Girl • My Heart Will Go on (Love Theme from *Titanic*) • Perfect • Roar • Rolling in the Deep • Say Something • Shake It Off • Some Nights • The Sound of Silence • Stay with Me • Sweet Caroline • Uptown Girl • What a Wonderful World • Yesterday • You've Got a Friend.

00275999 .... $9.99

Disney Songs for Ocarina
Arranged for 10-, 11-, and 12-hole ocarinas.

Be Our Guest • Bibbidi-Bobbidi-Boo (The Magic Song) • Can You Feel the Love Tonight • Chim Chim Cher-ee • Colors of the Wind • Do You Want to Build a Snowman? • Evermore • For the First Time in Forever • Hakuna Matata • He's a Pirate • How Does a Moment Last Forever • How Far I'll Go • I Just Can't Wait to Be King • In Summer • Kiss the Girl • Lava • Mickey Mouse March • Seize the Day • Supercalifragilisticexpialidocious • That's How You Know • When You Wish Upon a Star • Whistle While You Work • Who's Afraid of the Big Bad Wolf? • A Whole New World • Winnie the Poo • Yo Ho (A Pirate's Life for Me) • You Can Fly! You Can Fly! You Can Fly! • You're Welcome • You've Got a Friend in Me • Zip-A-Dee-Doo-Dah.

00275998 .... $9.99

WWW.HALLEONARD.COM

0318